The Encouragement Guide

An interactive journal to build healthy self-esteem & confidence for GIRLS

By Erika D. Johnson

The Encouragement Guide
An Interactive Journal to Build Healthy Self-Esteem & Confidence for Girls

ISBN 979-8-218-08294-9

Interior Design by Erika D. Johnson

The Encouragement Guide is a Beata Beatus Co. READ product.
For information about Beata Beatus READ, a division of Beata Beatus Co.
please visit www.beatabeatus.com.

blessed abundance

confidence love

I will go far

I am loved

royalty I am beautiful

ME vs Meee

I'm THAT GIRL

encourage I am enough

This Journal Belongs to 

____

LET'S KEEP GOING

This is Dedicated to You, Girl

Dear You,

My name is Erika, you can just call me E. Growing up as a young girl, I battled with the "enoughs" & the "toos." I wasn't good enough, this enough, or that enough. Or, I was too dark, too skinny, too tall or this & that. As I grew older, I learned that we all have gifts that we're meant to develop, use & share with the world & that those enoughs & toos were just there to try & make me feel like I was worthless & lower my self-esteem.

Today, I know that every detail about me, from my skin color & height to the tone of my voice was given to me on purpose to help me use my gifts. It's all connected & while you're still learning how your life will connect together, I wrote this journal to encourage & remind you that you're more than enough & too beautiful to not be your authentic self. If you want to know more about me & what I do, scan the code below.

Erika

Building your self-esteem can be tricky, so I want to make sure that I'm guiding & encouraging you throughout your journal. I'll share some quotes, stories, ask questions, there'll be arrows like the ones BELOW and

JOURNAL TIME

OR

JOURNAL

A space for you to write.

Anytime you see **LETTERS** you can always color them in.

ME, MYSELF & I

My nickname is (fill in the box)

____

My fav thing to do is

____

I LOVE that I am

____

My fav song is

____

AND A LITTLE MORE ... ME

I **LOVE** that I have

____

I wish that I could

____

I don't like that

____

I want to be able to do

____

facts
my fav
me, myself, & I
"I like..."

SELF-ESTEEM

When you think about yourself what is your opinion ?

Circle the words that you think / believe about yourself.
Make sure you're honest with yourself in choosing your words. You will use this later.

Do you like all of the words that you circled ?

Can you add more of your own words that better describe how you feel about yourself ?

Are the words mostly positive or negative in your opinion ?

Were you honest with yourself when circling your words ?

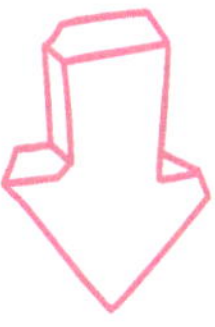

On the next page, journal the areas where you want to improve your self-esteem or your opinion about yourself.

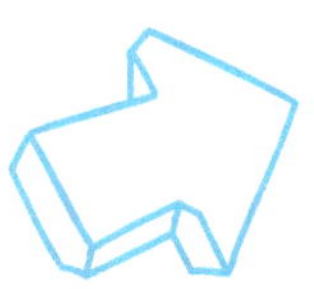

JOURNAL 

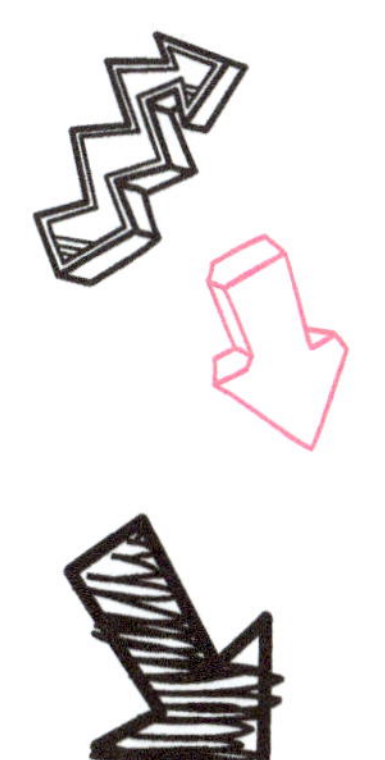

"I Love Myself"

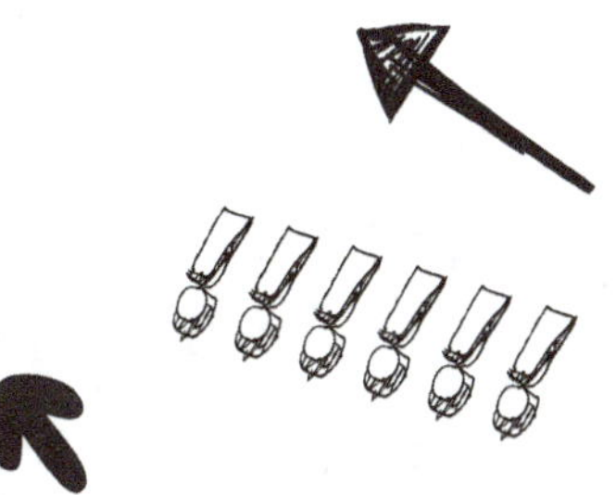

SELF-LOVE IS BETTER ...

If you could have as many likes & followers on your social media apps, how many would you want and why ?

It always feels good when someone gives us compliments, whether it's on a photo or a video we post or if they're complimenting our looks, outfit or personality but the most important ingredient to healthy self-esteem is how you love yourself even if you never get compliments.

DO YOU THINK GIRLS WHO TAKE SELFIES HAVE A HIGH OR LOW SELF ESTEEM ?

DOES THE AMOUNT OF PEOPLE WHO RESPOND TO WHAT YOU POST ON SOCIAL MEDIA AFFECT HOW YOU FEEL ABOUT YOURSELF ?

self-love tiktok love hearts selfie love

THAN SELFIE LOVE

**Strong Bold Smart Aggressive Emotional Sweet
Quiet Pretty Good Shy Silly Energetic Kind Loud Playful
Funny Popular Lame Nerdy Emo**

See if any words describe you, if not add your own.

BEST	GOOD	BAD	WORST

JOURNAL

Is there anything in your heart section that you want to change about yourself?

Journal how you can love yourself with all of your qualities, the good and bad ones.

____

____

____

____

____

____

____

____

____

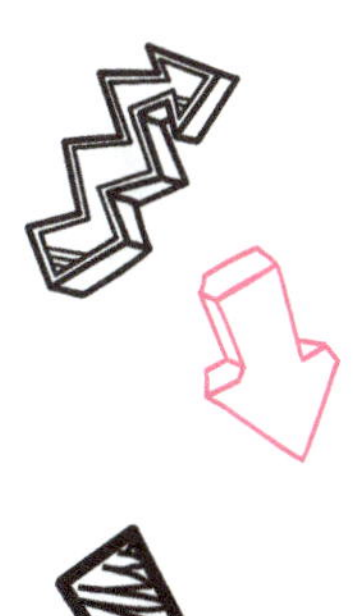

"SELF-LOVE IS BETTER THAN SELFIE LOVE"

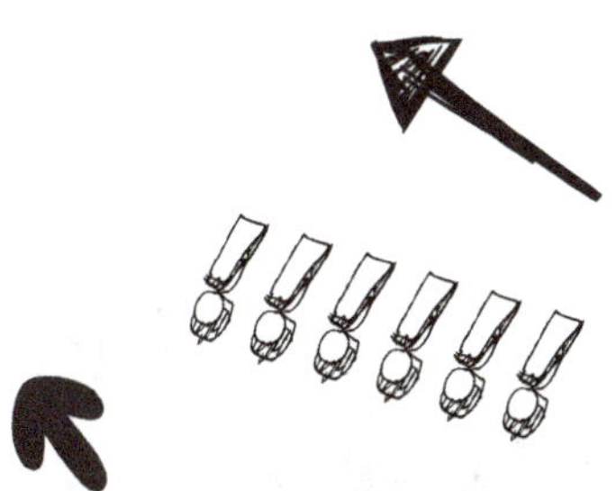

AUTHENTIC

BEING AUTHENTIC IS BEING YOUR TRUE SELF & NOT BEING AFRAID TO SHARE WHO YOU ARE WITH OTHERS.

Sometimes it's hard to be our true selves. The things that make us stand out can become things we try to hide or dislike about ourselves, especially if we are different than most people or don't like what's popular.

If you feel like you hate the things that make you stand out, remember that it sets you apart & that being different is OK. When you are authentic in who you are, you leave a mark in this world that no one else can.

BEING

AUTHENTIC

IS

COOL

Maybe you dress differently OR like a certain hobby.

It may be something small that you don't see others doing

BUT <u>do it</u> anyway !

When you are honest about who you are with yourself & others, you attract people who are meant to be in your life.

genuine confidence real original

BE REAL

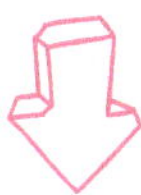

WHAT THINGS MAKE YOU FEEL EXCITED?

WHAT MAKES YOU FEEL GOOD WHEN DOING IT?

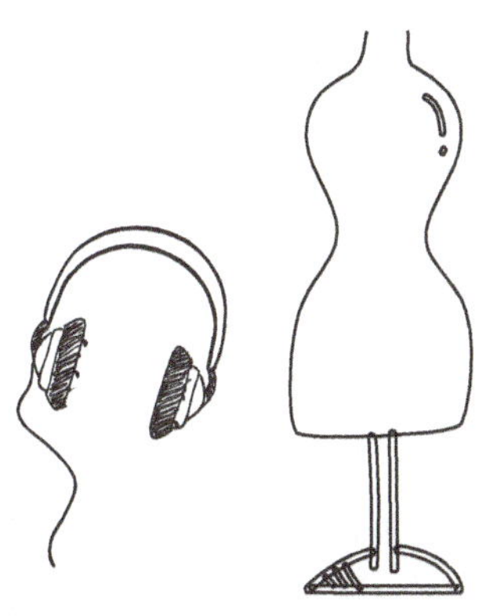

JOURNAL

Do you think you are authentic?
Do you change how you act or what you like based on who you're around?

Journal about the things that you like to do and why they make you happy.

____

____

____

____

____

____

____

____

____

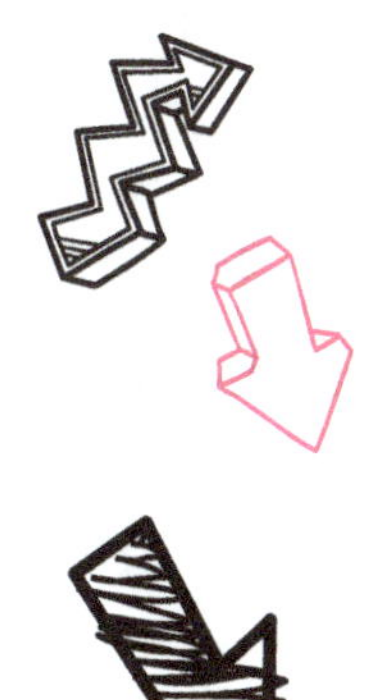

"I AM NOT AFRAID TO BE MY AUTHENTIC SELF"

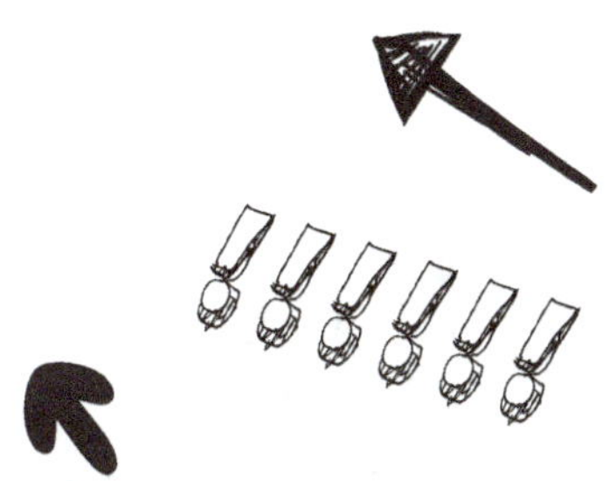

YOU'RE DESTINED TO GO FAR

I've traveled to a few countries & every time I go somewhere new, I learn about another culture, but I also learn something new about myself too.

I'VE LEARNED THAT I AM

BRAVE,
RESILIENT,
CREATIVE,

 & REALLY LOVE NATURE.

You don't have to travel to another country but as you travel through life, you'll learn about yourself in new ways.

Remember that no matter what you're faced with, you are destined to go far beyond your wildest dreams & that you can do anything that you put your mind to.

FINISH THE LIFE MAP, FILL IN WHERE YOU'RE FROM & WRITE DOWN YOUR GOALS. THESE CAN BE STATES, COUNTRIES, CAREERS OR SCHOOLS. THE CHOICE IS YOURS !

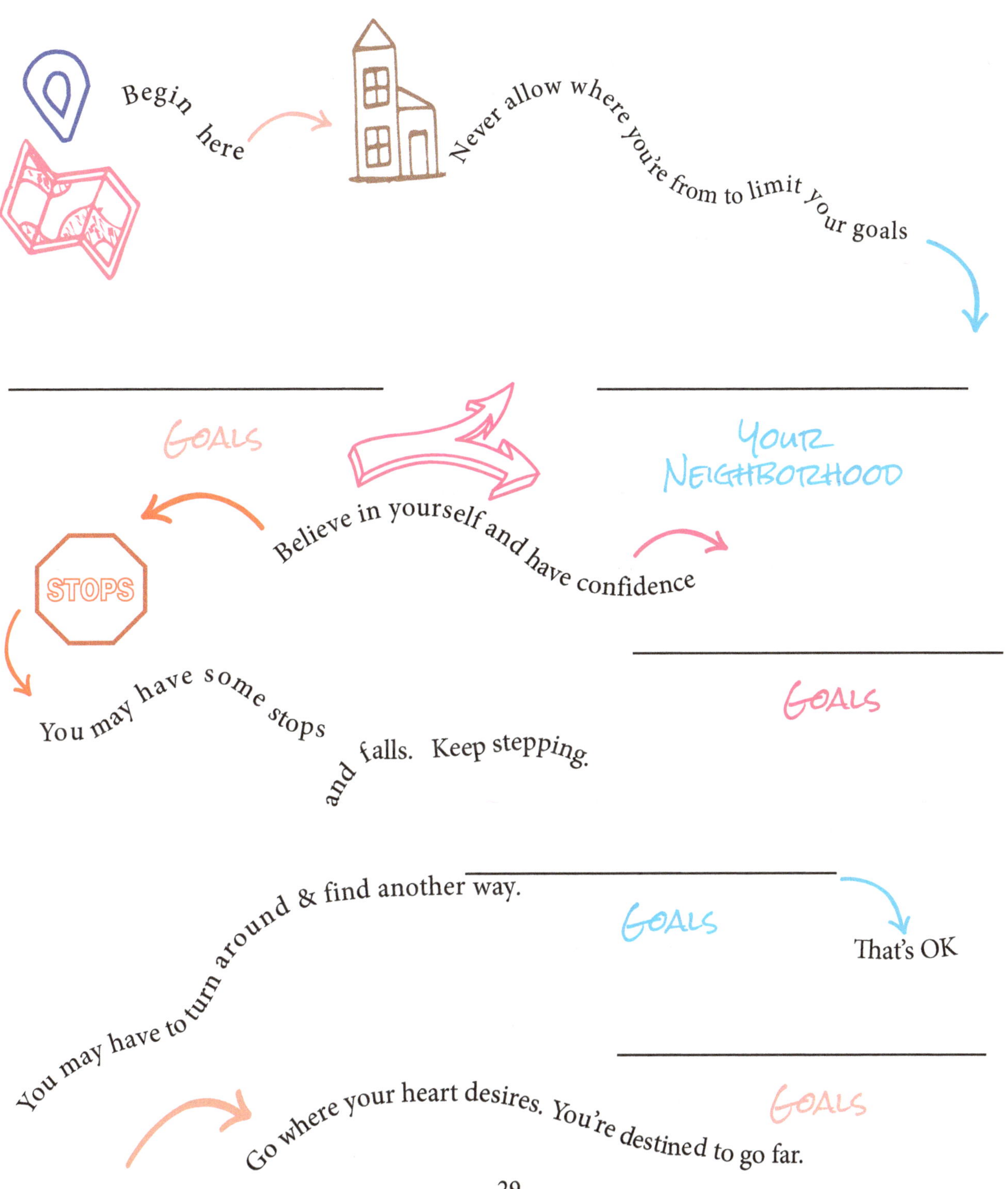

JOURNAL 

What are some goals that you have for yourself when you get older?

What things can you say to yourself now to help you reach your goals?

Journal what you want your life to look like in the future?

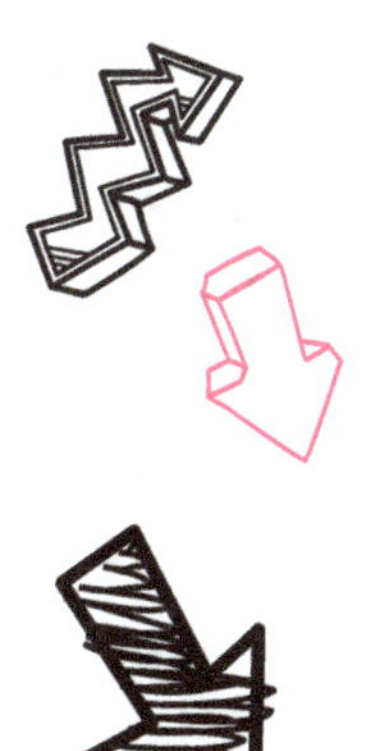

"MY FUTURE WILL BE BRIGHT"

THE RAREST DIAMOND

DIAMONDS ARE FORMED DEEP WITHIN THE EARTH BY TEMPERATURE & PRESSURE. SOME ARE FORMED IN MONTHS & OTHERS CAN TAKE HUNDREDS OF YEARS. DIAMONDS CAN COST UP TO MILLIONS OF DOLLARS AND SIMPLY BEGIN AS CARBON DEPOSITS FROM ORGANIC MATERIAL UNDERGROUND.

Nature shows us that it doesn't matter how you start & where you come from but that in due time, you will develop into the most amazing & precious jewel that you're destined to be.

Sometimes where we come from, how we begin OR past decisions can make us feel worthless.

I've made decisions & mistakes where I felt like I was worth nothing, but time has proven that there is nothing that can rob me of the truth.

That truth is the same for you ...

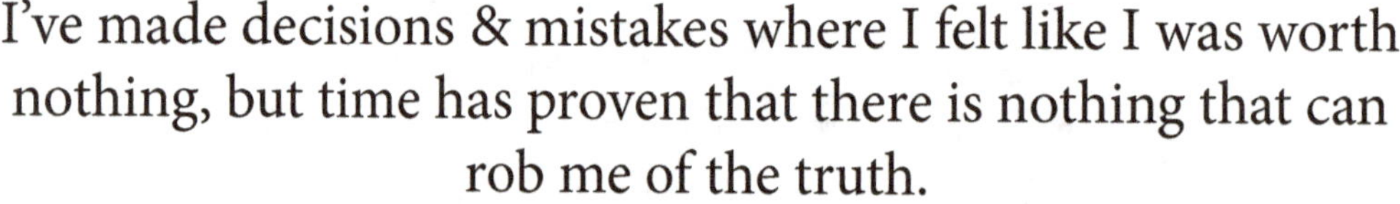

You are precious and rare, meant to glisten as you shine your light into the world.

WRITE DOWN SOME THINGS THAT ARE HARD IN YOUR LIFE,
OR THAT MAKE MAKE YOU FEEL HEAVY
AND UNDER PRESSURE.

Pressure Looks Like ...
Heaviness Feels Like ...

JOURNAL

Look at the words that you wrote down on the previous page.

Journal ways that you can overcome 'pressure' throughout your day.

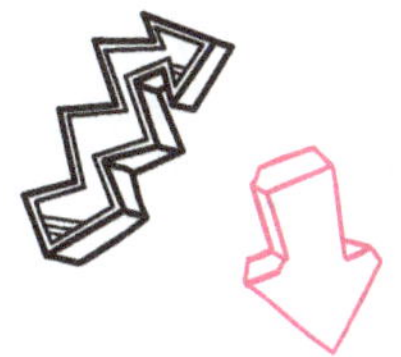
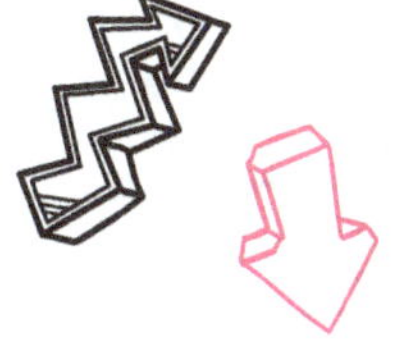

"TIME + PRESSURE CREATES DIAMONDS"

COLOR OUTSIDE THE LINES

When you color outside of the lines,
it might look bad, ugly or seem wrong.

When you take a pink, blue or green
crayon & go outside the thick black
lines, it may look crazy at first but
they eventually make up another black
line that someone else can create from.

Think of coloring outside the lines like thinking outside of the box. It may be scary, seem wrong or cause some stares, but when you think differently or color outside of the lines, you create new lines that others can see & create from. So be different, others will get inspired & begin to try different things too.

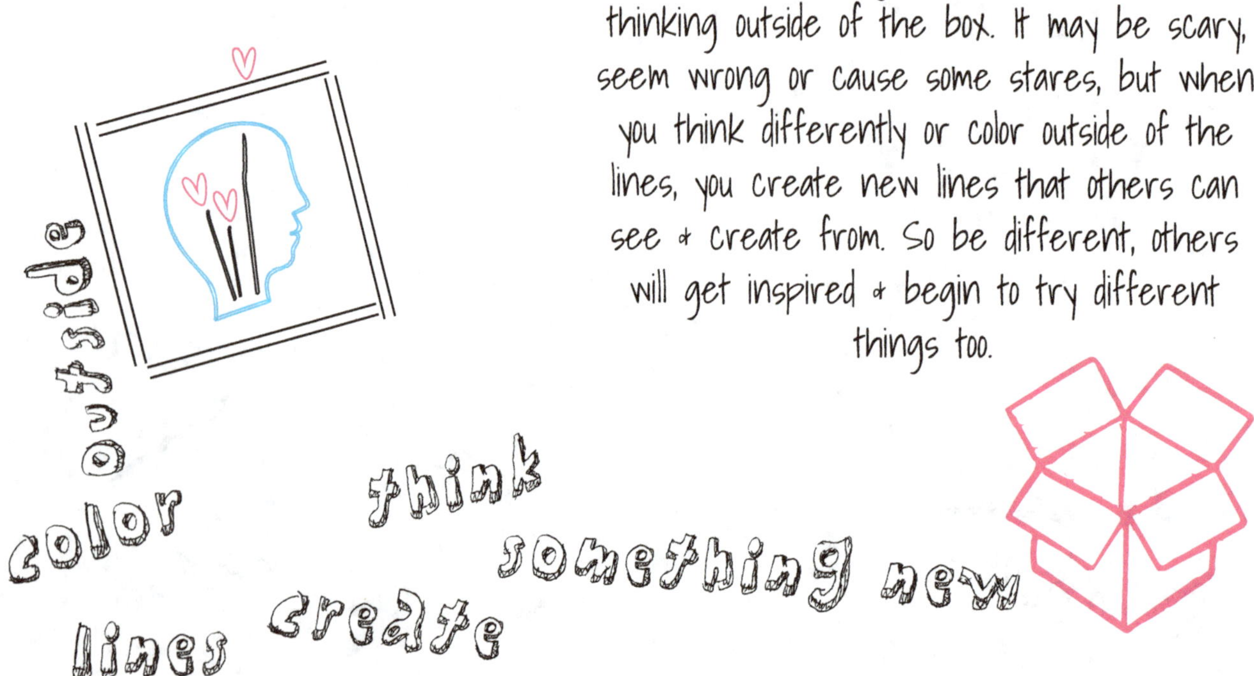

COLOR INSIDE OR OUTSIDE THE LINES. DRAW YOUR OWN.
& CREATE SOMETING NEW FROM THE PATTERNS

CREATIVITY

Free write some things that you want to do or would like to try, don't worry if it's never been done before.

Make this a safe space to be free with your creativity. There are no boundaries.

____

____

____

____

____

____

____

____

____

____

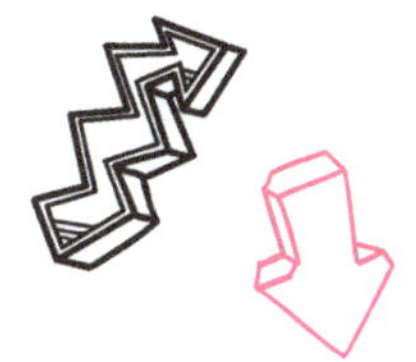

"GO OUTSIDE THE LINES, CREATE BOLDLY"

I'M THAT GIRL

I started writing poetry in grade school & when I was about 15 I wanted to create a blog. As I began searching for a blog name, I looked up words in different languages that represented what I wanted to be. I found the word "Beatus" which means blessed in Latin & I named my first blog "E beatus" which for me meant "E is blessed."

AT THE TIME, I DIDN'T REALIZE IT, BUT I WAS CALLING MYSELF WHAT I WANTED TO BE.

As a young girl, there are many things that others can call you, but let's focus on calling ourselves what we want to become. Over time, I've learned that it is very important to call yourself what you want to become in the future.

THAT GIRL

THAT GIRL

THAT GIRL

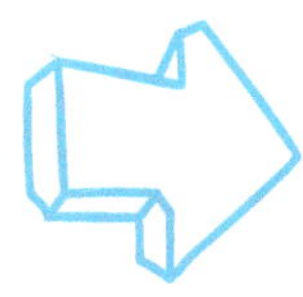

 JOURNAL

Take time to free journal & think about the best version of yourself, write down the details & include some of the words you wrote in the "THAT GIRL" section.

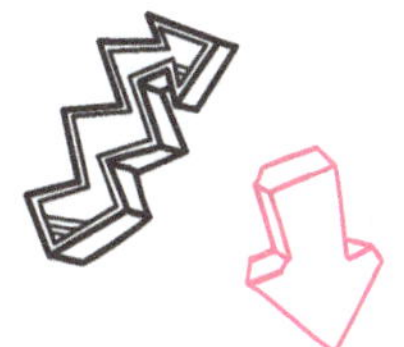

"I'M THAT GIRL"

POSITIVES + − NEGATIVES

FACT

UNDERSTANDING POSITIVES & NEGATIVES IS VERY IMPORTANT,
ONCE YOU DO, THINKING ON ONE OR THE OTHER CAN SHAPE YOUR
MINDSET AND ULTIMATELY YOUR LIFE.

There will always be something negative to think on & there will also always be something positive to think on. Choose to focus on the positive! Even if it makes no sense or is very hard to do. If all you can think about are negative things & words, it's OK, we can find the opposite & begin to train our minds to think on the

P O S I T I V E S

This is something that has helped to change my opinion about my life & my opinion about myself. My self-esteem changed when I started switching out my negative thoughts for positive ones.

good   hopeful   pessimistic   optimistic   focus   better

POSITIVE THINKING WORD SEARCH

Find the words in the puzzle. Words can go in any direction & can share letters as they cross over each other.

Appreciation	Attitude	Effort
Expectation	Focus	Hope
Improvement	Mindset	Optimism
Outlook	Peace	Perseverance
Positive	Resilient	Self
Talk	Thinking	Thoughts

```
B L K N A O A O K M E E L R G M Z U H M D N
Z O Q O C D D Q N N D X E C R S Y I T M Y P
P S S I B L D M U S S P G P I K F F S Z K
C L E T J E Z E T I I U O E F M G M Z V O G
Z Y V A V I D I E L M D I O C I A R T O B N
G M Q I B L T R I G Y E L F T T A F L H C I
E Y P C H T F E M J F V P O F P A T F S Y K
Y X Z E A F N N P Q W E G C O O U T G G F N
W Z F R R T B D K A Q B S U I O H D I R M I
M O H P N S P O N L C J E S N D B O H O H H
T J K P T N E M E V O R P M I Z I Z F B N T
J A L A U B W V N G X E P L T M Z B Y Z E Z
Y W X M V I O W E G V M W O P E A C E W O A
V Y W H K J A Z P R V K O A O N S K Z L K Y
K S O G N L S A P A A V T J S Q D D Z I S H
F L E S P X A H I D K N D G I T A Q N T D S
W J N Y I A O T T T S I C G T G X A H I Q G
I N N H M P S M M H G R O E I H Q G O Z M K
L N H D E D T D H Q Z D N P V U U Z X I B V
P K E S T S O G T P E A T E E O W U T U T W
E F F O R T W K M I U R V S H Y D F P M N Y
Y I E M Q L Z C Y G W U F T X H Y K H I I R
```

JOURNAL

Write down what positives you can switch out for any negatives that you have written about yourself previously in this journal.

You can go back to the self-esteem activity on page 10 to review what you've circled.

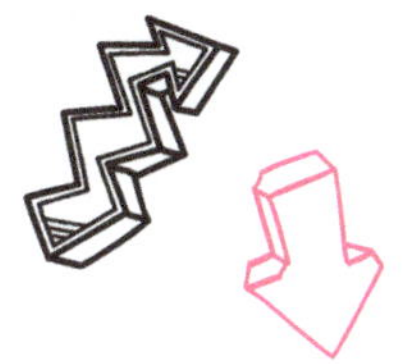

"FOCUS ON THE POSITIVE"

IN THE CLOUDS

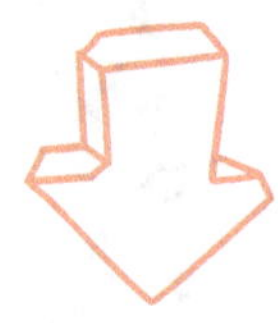

HAVING OUR HEADS IN THE CLOUDS IS NOT ALWAYS A BAD THING. AN IDEA CAN BECOME A VISION, AND THAT VISION BECOMES A DREAM THAT CAN COME TRUE.

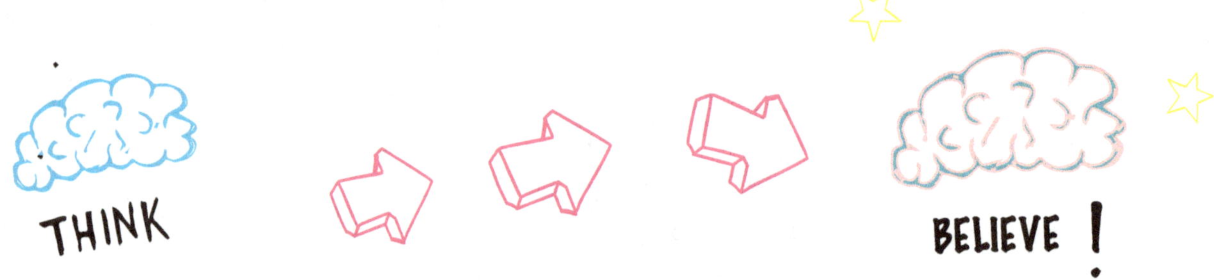

THE CHALLENGE BETWEEN YOUR IDEA PHASE & YOUR DREAM COMING TRUE LIES IN YOU BELIEVING IN YOURSELF.

Surrounding yourself with images & the knowledge of others who are making their dreams come true, will help you believe that it can happen for you too. So remember that every idea that you have is precious. Choose each one wisely & never stop dreaming.

PLACE SOME OF YOUR WILDEST DREAMS IN THE CLOUDS, USE A FEW WORDS TO DESCRIBE YOUR DREAM. IF YOU DON'T HAVE A DREAM, WRITE DOWN SOME IDEAS YOU HAVE. SEARCH PEOPLE ON THE INTERNET TO SEE WHO HAS ALREADY ACCOMPLISHED A SIMILAR IDEA OR DREAM THAT YOU HAVE.

Write down your wildest dreams. Go as far as you can, think big & then challenge yourself to think even bigger than that. What can you imagine yourself becoming & accomplishing? Share how inspiring & motivating it is to see other people accomplishing dreams that are similar to yours.

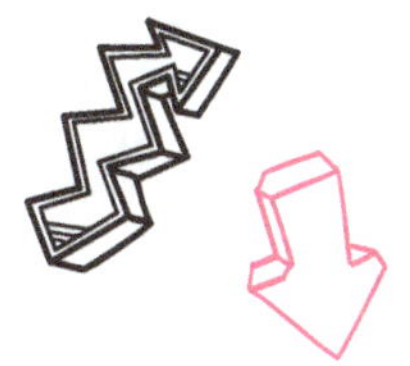

"HEAD IN THE CLOUDS"

MY NO BAGGAGE

ABUNDANCE - A VERY LARGE QUANTITY OF SOMETHING. AN OVERFLOWING FULLNESS; OR MORE THAN ADEQUATE QUANTITY OR SUPPLY.

Abundance may be a word you're not using often or at all but NOW is a great time to start.

NO DAMAGED GOODS ABUNDANCE BAG

FILL YOUR BAG WITH THINGS YOU WANT TO HAVE AN ABUNDANCE OF. YOU CAN WRITE WORDS, DRAW SYMBOLS OR PICTURES.

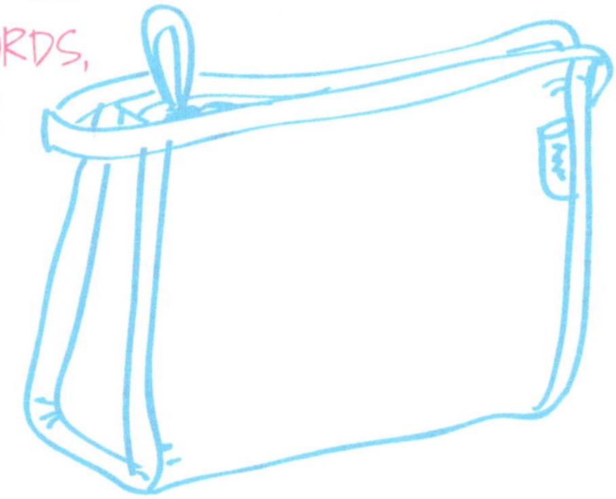

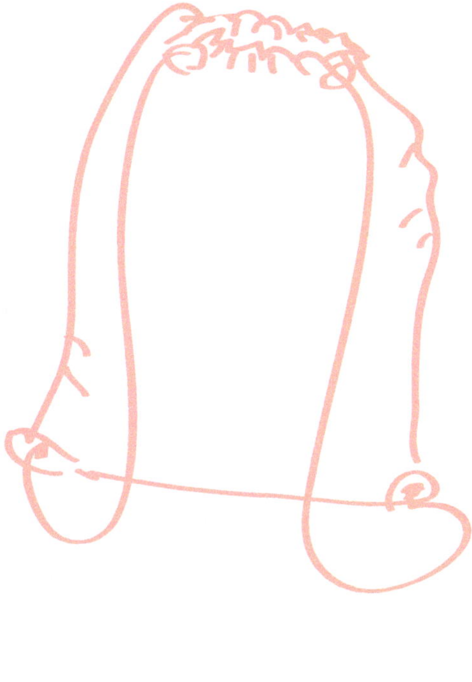

JOURNAL

What feels like baggage to you? Is there anything that you carry that you need to let go of? This can be something like remembering a bad situation or always feeling scared or anxious. Create 5 or more abundance affirmations. Start with,

I HAVE AN ABUNDANCE OF ...

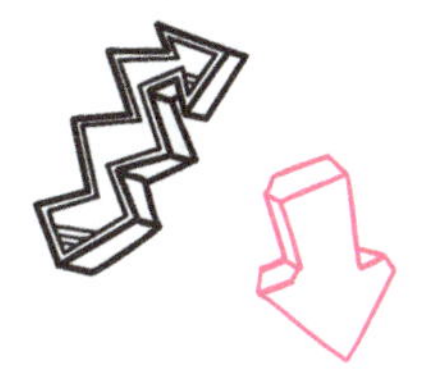

"IN MY ABUNDANCE BAG"

YOU vs. YOU

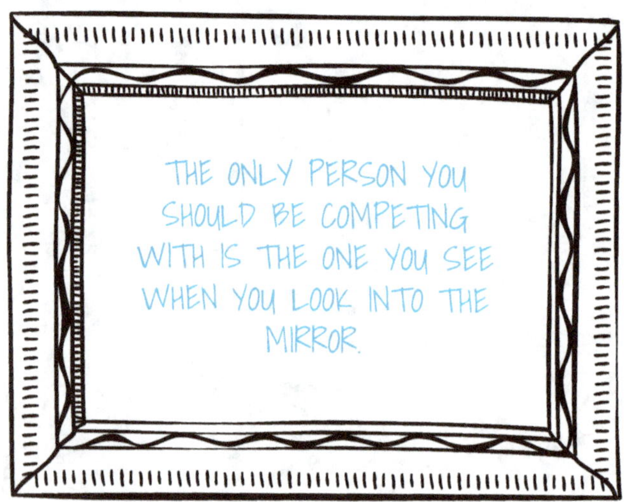

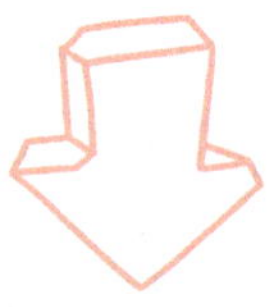

I AM BEAUTIFUL EVEN THOUGH I HAVE FLAWS

Let's prepare our minds to write down some affirmations that remind us of the best parts of ourselves and that push us to work on the parts that need a little improvement.

When you focus on improving & becoming better than you were the day before, it allows you to grow & stops you from comparing yourself to others.

JOURNAL

Some people write affirmations on a sticky note & place them on their mirrors in their room. How can you incorporate seeing your affirmations every day?

Everyone has flaws & improvements that need to be made. Never compare your good and bad parts to someone else's. It's You v.s You.

Write some affirmations down that will help you reach your full potential. Journal 5 affirmations that remind you who you are.

____

____

____

____

____

____

____

____

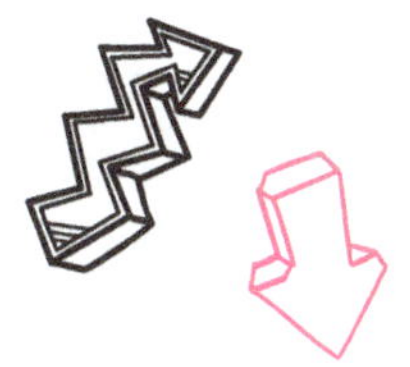

"COMPETING WITH THE OLD ME"

PLAY YOUR LIST

It's OK to feel how you feel & it's OK to have bad days. Sometimes the bad days & negative emotions are there to show us something that we need to focus our attention on to change.

Bad days can be there to show us things about ourselves that we need to work on or things to avoid & to not do again in the future.

When I experienced a very hard time in my life, I didn't want to do anything, talk to anyone or go anywhere. I was sad a lot and the one thing that helped me to release a lot of my feelings while seeing how I needed to change myself was listening to music with encouraging lyrics & free journaling my emotions.

PLAYLIST

PLAYLIST

Cranky

Disappointed

Lonely

Disgusted

Angry

Scared

Frustrated

Worried

Hurt

Sad

JOURNAL

Journal ways that you can make yourself feel better & boost your mood when you have bad days. You can write down reminders to think on or something funny that'll make you laugh like a memory or a scene from a movie.

____

____

____

____

____

____

____

____

____

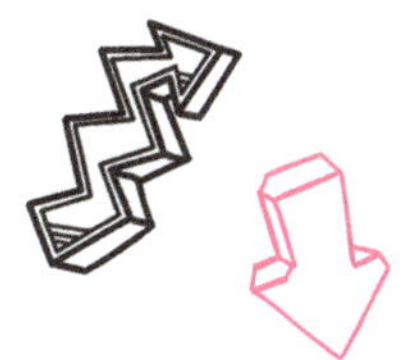

"IT'S OK TO HAVE BAD DAYS"

FREE JOURNAL

FACT

FREE JOURNALING IS A PERSONAL RECORD OF EXPERIENCES & REFLECTIONS KEPT ON A REGULAR BASIS.

Sometimes **free journaling** when you're upset helps you. However, you don't need to be upset to free journal.

When you free journal, you release all emotions especially negative ones & it is cathartic for you.

That's right, a catharsis or to feel cathartic is to have an emotional release. You can get psychological relief through writing & express very strong emotions as if you were screaming or crying.

RULE #1

THERE ARE NONE

WRITE WHATEVER IS ON YOUR MIND.

THIS IS SCIENTIFICALLY PROVEN !

FROM HERE ON OUT, THIS JOURNAL SPACE IS FOR YOU TO FREE JOURNAL.

FROM MY PERSONAL EXPERIENCE, THE MORE I JOURNAL, THE BETTER I FEEL, EVEN IF IT'S JUST FOR 5 MINUTES.

A Final Note From the Author

I hope that this journal has guided you to see how amazing you are & has encouraged you to continue to believe it as you navigate through your life. No matter what, remember to choose to fall in love with who you are every single day, the good & the bad parts of you. Life can happen fast. It was only yesterday (not really) when I was a teenager so don't forget to make memories, sit down, take a deep breath, journal your days & record how you feel. Soon you will look back, smile & see just how far you've come.

About the Author

Erika Johnson, a Pittsburgh native, is a writer, musician, entrepreneur and singer-songwriter; with a passion for encouraging others through creative expression in music & writing. In 2015 she created Beata Beatus Co. a company that began as a T-shirt line & as it evolves, she continues to create products for youths & young adults while using her story and life's experiences as tools to help heal & motivate those around her.

Learn more at www.erikadenaej.com

9 798218 082949